THIS BOOK BELONGS TO:

_____

HOW MANY FAVORITES WILL YOU SEE?

To my kids, friends and family who helped me along the way.

All rights reserved. This book or parts thereof may not be reproduced in any form, stored in any retrieval system, or transmitted in any form by any means—electronic, mechanical, photocopy, recording, or otherwise—without prior written permission of the publisher, except as provided by United States of America copyright law.

Portions of this book are works of fiction. Any references to historical events, real people, or real places are used fictitiously. Other names, characters, places and events are products of the author's imagination, and any resemblances to actual events or places or persons, living or dead, is entirely coincidental.

ISBN-13: 978-1725636644

First Printing 2018

Ndemediagroup.com

I am Abu the Antelope

I live in places where I can find plenty of grass to eat. I roam with my herd to keep me safe. With my long legs, I can leap and run fast to escape lions and crocodiles. My sharp horns help me defend myself.

I am Bobo the Baboon

I am a big monkey with large teeth. I live in the forest where I love to climb trees. My red buttocks will make you smile but I can sit for hours keeping watch. When I am hungry, I wander the grasslands looking for leaves, roots and seeds. I also like to eat insects and fish.

I am Croco the Crocodile

I am the largest reptile in Africa. I am one of the oldest animals on the planet. I live beside rivers and I hide in muddy water ready to pounce on my prey. My sharp teeth and strong jaws make me a feared hunter.

I am Diara the Dragonfly

I start life as a nymph and I live underwater. I leave the water to change into a dragonfly. You can see me flying around lakes and ponds with my sparkly wings. I eat mosquitoes, flies and bees. I live for only two weeks as a dragonfly!

I am Elroi the Elephant

I live in the African bush. I am the largest land animal in the world. My big ears keep me cool in the summer heat. I eat leaves and bark that I strip from trees and bushes with my long trunk. I also like juicy fruits and roots. I can drink 50 gallons of water a day sucked up through my trunk. I greet my friends by flapping my ears and trumpeting!

I am Fynn the Frog

I am an African clawed frog with sharp claws that I use to hunt. I can swim fast. I feed on insects, spiders, worms, bugs and small fish. I live in the bottom of lakes and rivers. I only come to the surface to breathe. My green-grey skin helps to hide me from other animals.

I am Gisele the Giraffe

I am the world's tallest animal. With my long neck, I can see further than any other land animal. When my babies are born, they are taller than a fully grown person! I can reach leaves in treetops that other animals cannot reach. Acacia leaves are my favorite. My legs are very powerful and I can kill a lion with one kick.

I am Hadee the Hippopotamus

I live in rivers, lakes and swamps.
I have a large body and huge head with
stumpy legs. I am often called a 'water
horse'. To keep cool, I wallow in mud or
I lie in water with only my eyes, ears and
nostrils showing. I can hold my breath for
five minutes! At night when it is cooler,
I eat grass using my lips to pull it up.

I am Itri the Impala

I am Itri the Impala. I am a member of the antelope family. I like to eat grass, shoots and leaves. My curved horns grow up to three feet long to show other impalas how strong I am. I use my long horns to fight off lions, cheetahs and crocodiles.

I am Jengo the Jackal

I am Jengo the Jackal. I am similar to a dog but my night-time call is loud and shrill. I sleep during the day in my den or under rocks where it is cool. I look for food at night. I eat plants and small animals but you can often see me with lions. I feed on what is left of their prey.

K KUDU

I am Kia the Kudu

I am Kia the Kudu. I live in grasslands and woodlands. The stripes on my body help me to blend in with the bushes when I am hiding from lions. I eat leaves, flowers, berries and fruits. Some people think I am a sacred animal and they protect me.

I am Lewa the Lovebird

I am a small and colorful parrot. I search for food with my flock. We eat seeds and berries we find in the forests and fields. I build my nest in a hole in a rock or a tree. When I find a mate, we stay together for life. You might see us sleeping side by side!

I am Matt the Meerkat

I live in the hot desert. I eat insects, lizards and rodents. I sniff out my prey and then I dig it from the sand.
I live in a group and we take turns keeping watch. We stand on our hind legs and peer around. When we see a hawk, jackal, or snake, we call to other meerkats. Then we all dive into our burrow!

I am Neo the Nyala

I am a striped antelope with long twisty horns. My favorite place to live is in the grasslands near a river. I spend the day resting in nearby woodlands. At night, I come out to feed on lush grass. I also eat seeds and fruits. I like to show off my shaggy coat and my long horns to other male nyala.

I am Obi the Ostrich

I am the world's largest bird and we lay the largest eggs. I have a long neck and a small head with big eyes and thick lashes. I eat plants and sometimes insects. Like all birds, I do not have teeth. I swallow pebbles or grit to help me grind my food. Although I cannot fly, I am the fastest bird on land. I can run almost as fast as a lion! I have a powerful kick.

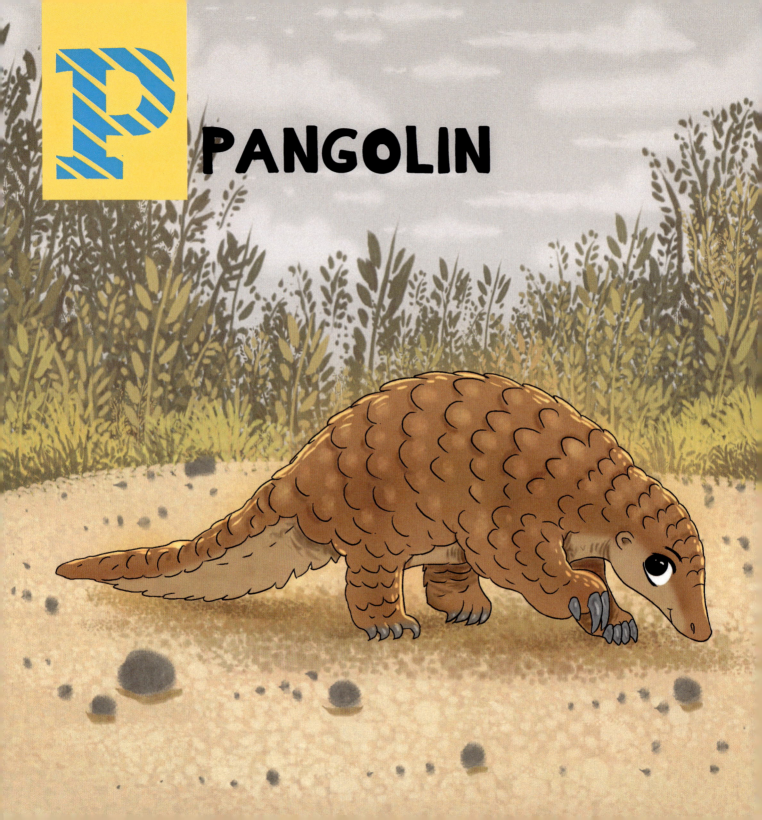

I am Polo the Pangolin

I live in forests and swamps. I can swim and climb trees. I am the only mammal with scales on my body. I eat termites that I dig from the ground with my sharp claws. I cannot see very well so I use my ears, nose and long tongue to find my way. When I am scared, I let off a foul smell and curl into a ball!

I am Qaree the Quail

I am a small bird from the pheasant family. I eat grains, fruits, grasshoppers and worms. I spend a lot of time on the ground. I only fly a short way. I am hunted by hawks, snakes, squirrels, rats, dogs and cats. I always hide so they can't catch me!

R RHINOCEROS

I am Rabee the Rhinoceros

I live in grassy places with trees and bushes. I have a huge body, short legs and two horns on my snout. I live alone and I eat plants, shoots and fruits. My eyesight is poor but I can hear and smell very well. I can even tell how old another black rhino is just by smelling their dung!

I am Sefu the Snake

My skin is brown or grey but the inside of my mouth is black. That is why everyone calls me the black mamba snake. I live on the ground and I eat small mammals and birds.

I can grow to 14 feet long. I am the fastest African snake and the most feared. I am very poisonous. I hide from people but if I am scared, two drops of my venom can kill a person.

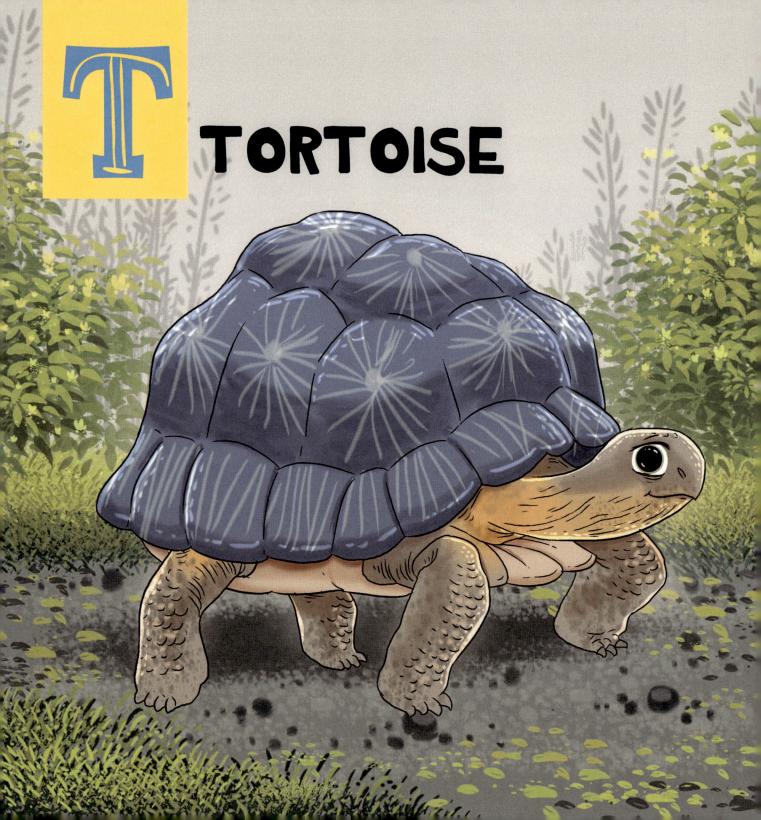

I am Tammy the Tortoise

I am an African-spurred tortoise
and I live in the dry. I am the third largest
tortoise in the world. I am a reptile with a
hard shell and softer belly, head and legs.
I move very slowly. When I am afraid,
I pull my head and legs into my shell.
I bask in the morning sun to warm up.
When it is hot, I go underground.
I can live up to 150 years!

I am Umi the Uromastix

I am a lizard and I live in dry areas of North Africa. I am one foot long with a stout body and spiked tail. I lash out when animals come into my burrow. I eat plants. Sometimes I eat insects and even young lizards! I spend my days basking in the sun or hiding underground.

I am Venda the Vulture

I am a large, odd looking bird with a bald head, loose skin and a sharp curved beak. You can find me flying over desert and grasslands. I do not kill my own food. I am a scavenger. I have very good eyesight and I can spot dead animals from a few miles away!

I am Wasee the Warthog

I am like a pig but my snout has two warts and two tusks. I live in grasslands close to water where I can drink and wallow to keep cool. I eat grass, roots, berries and insects that I dig up with my tusks. I live in family groups called 'sounders'.

I am Xola the Xerus

I am an African ground squirrel.
I am a rodent with sharp teeth.
I eat roots, seeds, grains, fruits, insects
and eggs. My teeth do not stop growing
but I wear them down when I eat.
When I am out of my burrow, my bushy
tail shades my back from the sun.

I am Yaro the Yellow-Winged Bat

I am a flying mammal. I have yellow ears, nose and wings. I live close to acacia trees and thorn bushes. I eat insects. I use my long ears to listen for them flying past and I chase them. I roost in small trees and shrubs. When I find a mate, we pair up for life.

I am Zahra the Zebra

You can find me roaming the grasslands with my herd. I am like a horse but I have black and white stripes. We all have a unique pattern, like people have unique fingerprints. Our stripes make it hard for a lion to pick one of us out from the herd. I sleep standing up!

Other books by Fleurie Leclercq

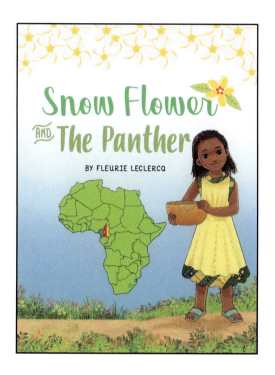

Snow Flower
And The Panther

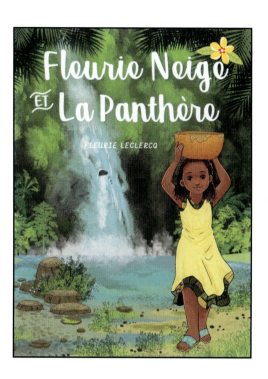

Fleurie Neige
Et La Panthère

Visit our site
www.snowflowerbooks.com
and print your coloring pages for free

Made in the USA
San Bernardino, CA
01 March 2020